First Sight

First Sight

Kevin Patrick Sullivan

MILLE GRAZIE PRESS
Santa Barbara

Published by Mille Grazie Press
PO Box 92023, Santa Barbara, California 93190

Library of Congress Catalog Card Number 94-79189
ISBN 0-9638843-4-4

The author and publisher would like to express their grateful acknowledgment to the following publications in which some of these poems first appeared: The Backyard Press, The Practical Mystic, Cafe Solo, Poets & Paupers, Coffeehouse Poets Quarterly, Hot Coffee, Myth, Earth Words *(White Crow Press),* Shadows *(Deertree Press),* Offering the Throat *(Café Solo Press).*

"Summer of Drought" was published as a broadside from Sand River Press and Phoenix Books; "A Thin Blue Line," "Yearning," and "Passing," were first published as broadsides from Garden Street Press.

Acknowledgments:
There are many people to whom I owe allegiance and gratitude: none more than to my sisters, Ann, Patty, Carol and Rose; Karl and Ruth Kempton; Linnaea Phillips; Will Inman; Hernán Castellano-Girón; Kate Harper; Benjamin Saltman; Nicholas Campbell; Marguerite Costigan; my editors and publishers, Cynthia Anderson and David Oliveira; and Cathy and Kara Carwise.

For my mother and father
who started it
and kept it going

For Cathy and Kara
who continue it

CONTENTS

Kevin's Tree

for Kevin Patrick Sullivan

1

sometimes he feels like a tree. he stretches
on his back on a roof, painting an overhang.
dark oil-base paint drips on his face, in his
hair, down his arms. he feels like wood given
dark stain.

          but his tree lives, his wood's
still growing. roots lift out through him into
sky, limbs burrow through his feet, his shoes,
into earth. all air knows enters his invisible
darkthrusts. all that's in earth speaks to him
through limb-resonance. his dark lifethrob
reaches touch all that he is beyond him. he
roots in an orbit of waking. leaves sing

2

as we root into sky, so does sky grow
steep pace deep down us. our trees
and trees of heaven mingle, root and branch,
dark with each other's dormant light, those
rhythms touch tip fingers of dancing
principalities, angels with gravities of
joy setting free as they draw in. Kevin,
lying stained and sweaty on that roof,
feels his tree stir with oracle breath,
even his paintstrokes enter that healing
angel-dance, nothing he does can break
his communing bardic beat, all Erin's holy
trees speak in his woke song's laughing

Will Inman
26 August, 1989

FOREWORD

Kevin Patrick Sullivan's **FIRST SIGHT** is just that. **First** can be translated **genesis** and **original**: what is **seen** with new vision **generates** and **originates**. But Kevin says **First Sight**. He does not drag in complicated literary or intellectual **secondhand** terms. He looks out at a broken world and goes to beginnings, to essentials, to **elements**. 'It started in my hands...' but he does not brag: 'My song is thin...these words hardly pile up before they blow away.' His elements, I promise you, are as evanescent as sea-waves and mountains; he builds his music 'intoning the rhythms of sea, the cycle of night and day...song and dance joined in the birth of a line.' 'The silence fills itself with life, its voice combines remembrance and things yet unmade.' His elements work in paradoxes of nature: 'This field is my healing bed...my house of stone.' ' And what they are is already too huge to imagine.' 'You must pull it from its pockets you must shoulder it you must call it down upon you but you must not wait.' 'So I stand in the cold wind not able to think of you then luckily I awake and say your name — the sound brings us both to life.' 'Over the span of a day I breathe you again and again the world comes to me molecule by molecule this life my life becomes everything that breathes.'

The poet recalls to focus the elements-in-motion of what-is, beyond the clutter and cynicism of modern habits, he names what is important, what is first hand, what is **so**.

The naming of essentials, the renewal of clear focus on natural events and relationships, the raw fact of mortality, the immanence of cosmic connecting — all these emerge in these very simple — but not simplistic — poems. When Kevin speaks what has come to seem cliché, listen again: he restores the sounds to nature: not even air and dead leaves can stay cliché in the free grasp and firm letting-go of his knowing hands.

The finest poets do not settle for ornate vocabularies, nor for pastel phrases, nor for suave side-steps of a cannibal world — the finest poets restore us to living fundamentals, **first sight** of human and natural rhythmic events.

Kevin Patrick Sullivan has brought us, not backward to some fantasy Eden, but inward, central, to that true garden of Self that awaits our recognition and nurture. He gives us awake to the living trees of our own real selves.

Will Inman
30 August, 1994
Tucson

I am certain of nothing but the
holiness of the Heart's affections,
the truth of Imagination.

John Keats

First Sight

It started in my hands
those eyes of the flesh
so sure of what they feel
my fingers pushing the pen
toward open unknown space
ingesting this world
from where I first
picked it up

All Day Long

All day long
they pass
they point
they wonder what kind of man lives there
broken windows
plastic flapping
things untouched in the yard
no direction or plan of accomplishment
it looks like no one at all lives there
or maybe
someone at home
in the stubbornness of things
someone able to say
what I have
is what I found

A Thin Blue Line

Red — bright red against the clouds
a cardinal sits high
wavering with the wind

Such a thin blue line
circles the top of the world

Field Poem

This field in its lush winter green
leaps laughs shouts with the promise of seed
its joy fractures the sky at every grass blade's edge
this field   this field is my healing bed
my house of stone

Clouds

Walking the beach
it is evening
the clouds crest the nearby hills
and move inward
The light illumines them
making them appear
something other
than what they are
and what they are
is already
too huge
to imagine

A Summer of Drought

Under the silence of stars
nights unalterably long
this dry field waits

There has been no relief
from the wind
just the high pressure of the sun
smothering the days

My tears
would soften the earth
if I could only cry
until the lightning strikes

You Must Never Wait

You must pull it from its pockets
you must shoulder it
you must call it down upon you
but you must never wait

The rain comes to those who call it
who dance upon the wind
upon the dry earth
upon the seeds of their belief

You must call it down upon you
you must shoulder it
you must pull it from its pockets
but you must never wait

River Rising

The days crack
lightning crosses hillsides
thunder is the voice of the river
whose rage opens the fields of men
the river's dream is incessant
shapeless
the barest whisper of madness
escapes

Clouds

Have you noticed the clouds
invited them into your
space

It is almost
like having your lover
over for tea

The Wind

There has been no sound
for days
no word of my lover
her cave of silence
makes a tinderbox
of my heart

Vibrations

It is cold and windy in this dream
the sun has yet to shine
the clouds — a layered quilt
are just too thick

My heart is numb
your absence has smothered me
I have no feeling other than missing you

I would walk but the sky is too big
everywhere it is the same
without you

So I stand in the cold wind
not able even to think of you
then luckily I awake and say your name
the sound brings us both
to life

Landing in Detroit

My mind reaches back
across the width of this land
back to the feel of my fingers
in your hair
your head in my hands

There will be no slaking this thirst
the dream of you
stands so clear
my heart jumps
my hands trace your shape
in thin air

Over the Span of a Day

Over the span of a day
I breathe you again
and again the world
comes to me
molecule by molecule
this life my life
becomes everything
that breathes

Fixed Bath

Wrapped in silver
I can't see the picture
develop behind your eyes
what is it one must speak
to enter your dark room
lips smiling in song
words already forgotten
and when I learn the language
will you speak to me
in shades of black and white
negatives untouched by color
or any distraction of light

Anticipation

Your dream crashes against me
I am breathless
crushed by your beauty
I stumble towards acceptance
the shaping of a new word
useless

I am not struck dumb
just shy
after all how does one say
hello

You

You are the dawn burst
the full moon howl
the green buds of spring
you are the rainbow

Never Far

I have come to this beach, knowing
I would not find you
only trace your steps
that have washed away
still I feel closer to you
having done such a little thing
walking here where you used to

Blue Sky

There is something big as the sky inside you
a blue cloudless sky
an ocean inside you

Have you heard it move
along the lines of your eyes
felt it run the heart's valley
crest its snowy peaks

Have you dreamed inside your waking
that sound so silent
you know you're not alone

There is something big as the sky inside you
a blue cloudless sky, an ocean
inside you are the dreams
I look for in my waking
inside you I know
I will meet myself

Taffy Pull

In your long slender gait
traveling across my heart
you wind yourself and others
taffy being pulled
stretched   thinning
glossed over
with a sheen of ultimate
hardness

I've seen my own undoing
passed back and forth
candy for everyone

A World of Good

The corn is nearly four feet tall
already the wind is dry
its coming and going just marks time
the Fourth of July is next week
how long has it been
since you walked down the rows
felt the earth under your feet
scratched at the ground with your toes

Remember the feel of corn silk
how you used to laugh
we're going to have a picnic
you really should try to make it
it would do us all a world of good

Yearning

I dream your healing touch
what it must be like to meet inside
to rise and fall with a sharing of breath
to reach into the dark
and move as one dancing body
of light

In the Dark

We rage against the illusion of separateness
against the harsh realities of blind light
soothed and stroked by one pair of hands
it is silence that binds us
one to the other
inseparable in the dark

Praise Song

We lay bone to bone
long before this shape took flesh
hidden in the dark earth
we called forth this body
to absorb light

We are what each makes
of the light and dark

A two-edged sword
of indifference and intent
a lifting up into song
of one in praise of the other

The Night Sky

The night sky
threads the eye
ever upward

Where is the heart's limit

The Wind Circles Our Days

The wind circles our days
spiraling
the shadow of our descent never
lighting
always we are strangers in the garden
one after another turning stones
what we have is not enough
somehow somewhere
something else will matter
the wind circles
our days spiral one after another
we are lost
without ever leaving home

Red Moon

A slash of red horn
hangs in the night sky
this dream is too fragile
the color of blood
reminds me how precious
life is

Momentum

It must be the end
of the chain
what lies out beyond
is only imagined
until one is loosed
clawing through new ground
under an untethered sky
the future and the past
spin in this present
as all things spin
around what we don't know
or can't remember
it is like a whisper
that soft calling we feel
with the morning's breath
on our necks

Something in us
wants to leave
what we are

Two Men on the Edge of a Crowd

Each has a lapful
of dead leaves
out of season they cull the world
not for damaged or overripe fruit
what catches their eye
is the young and firm
the bright shiny green leaves
full of the promise
of shade

Signs Along the Road

Everywhere I look
the signs are too big
nothing is small when it comes to money
or bright enough
choose me they scream
a song from bitter lips

Passing

In the flight of a falcon
spiraling above me
I feel your somber eyes
tear at my breath

It is a cold wind
you ride
but I am not afraid

Dive from your terrible heights
join with me in this lonely field
talons and wings
arms and hands
each taking what they need

No Gentle Reminder

I feel the hawk's wings
tear at my breast
her breath
moist upon my flesh
her stare
hot in my heart

This is no gentle reminder
life is what life does
fear not the harvest of seed
for I am grounded in blood
through bone I take shape
I am an animal that howls
with the gift

Manna

A crow comes for breakfast
one large black bird
stalking the newly disked field
the message he brings
is one of hunger
the daily virtue of taking only
what is needed

The Crow is not a Broken Moon

The crow is not a broken moon
he is whole
whole as any one of us
a dark spot on the horizon
nothing else
is himself
a gift
unlike the tightly wrapped
black mass of fear
he so often calls to mind

Mustard and Lupine

Like the native peoples before them
their dance diminishes each year
on these central coast slopes
you begin to understand their reach
their explosion into color

Within our narrowing lifescapes
who accomplishes more

The Children Speak

The bones of their children scream at me

A star's cold grip turns me around
as a grandfather grabs my left arm

and the bones of their children scream at me

Leading my feet on a path
through this now open graveyard
protecting me from harm

and the bones of their children scream at me

As he gives me these words for the living
"the voices of all children
will be raised as one"

and the bones of our children scream at me

"See the torn open earth
look—what you have done"

This poem came into being after a walk through a burial site of the Chumash Indians that had been scraped and exposed by a land development on the coastal plain in Pismo Beach.

Animal Play

I have felt the heat of weightlessness
as if I could walk on water
shimmer in air
ride the breath where it wills
yet I choose to stay at surf's edge
play with dogs and sea otters
dance in the warm evening light
nurse as mammals do — on
mother's milk

| *Shadows* | *Las sombras* |

Spanish translation by Antonieta Olivares

There is	Hay
a relationship	una relación
between the Muse	entre la Musa
and the Word	y la Palabra
one the shadow	ser la sombra
of the other	la una de la otra

***

I can't	No puedo
believe	creer
what my ears	lo que mis oidos
see	ven
what my eyes	lo que mis ojos
hear	escuchan

***

Following	Siguiendo
the wild	a los gansos
geese	silvestres
I am	empiezo
beginning	a sentirme
to feel trapped	atrapado
locked	encerrado
in these	en los
patterns	moldes
year after	año tras
year	año

A Painter's Memory

Sometimes I feel like a tree
lost in my veins
banging my head in the wind
the oils that dapple my flesh
remind me of how I once
stood in the rain

Patience

I have held this rock
its shape
so well formed in the memory
of my hand
it has touched in me
basalt
quartz
molten lava
and
stone cold indifference

Moment By Moment

There are 86,400 seconds in a day
any one of which
can turn my life around

It is not so much the answers
as the questions

The questions must be right
from the inner source
from a distance
an observed action calmly
measuring out my heartbeats
to eternity

86,400 times a day

Everyday Living

The wash hangs out to dry
flaps in a smoke-filled breeze
contradictions appear

My pillows confused about the light
chatter in a nervous tongue
alien to themselves

My boots start a tentative dance
out of step with the previous moment
laughter echoes across the field

My palms break out in a sweat
static electricity charges forward
smiling expectantly

The light begins to burn brighter
shadows flee — finally fade
there's a flash of clarity

I recognize the smoke for what it is
the chaff of desire
the politics of everyday living

Poem

In the beginning song was mute
till the heart gave it wings
the voice of its freedom
a flutter
a cry of amazement

The sound of the heart
became the beating of drums
limbs moving out and away
and back again
intoning the rhythms of sea
the cycle of night and day

The word swirled in this matrix
pulsed and pushed into meter
song and dance joined
in the birth of a line
the making of a poem

Silence Strengthens the Word

Here in the midst of October
my pen begins to dry up
it prepares to quiet itself
to accept the slumbering of winter

Often in January it stirs
harboring strength from the silence
it begins to remember the dream
to gather itself for the wakening

About April there's a resurrection
the silence fills itself with life
its voice combines remembrance
and things yet unmade

Come July the dream is in focus
my pen is sure of what it's about
a mirror-image of life in bloom
the song sings itself

Rising

1

Language falls like rain
all its clamoring sounds
struggle to exist
to be remembered
where have we come from
where might we be going
how shall we get there

2

Rain all about me
confused clamoring sounds
struggle to be remembered
I whisper your name
over and over
the syllables
strike clarity
away from any answers
away from any questions
no direction but the present
lifting my face to yours
the sound of your breath covers my lips

3

Struggling sounds
clamor to exist
like rain washed away
never to be remembered
there is no more serious danger
than thinking we live forever
raise your voice with the birds the wind
the wolf and the sea
the drum of your heart beating
a joyful noise
the language of the world
pressed against your breast

4

Language rises like the day
the night
an offering
a kiss between lovers
grabbing bits and pieces
I make this world moment by moment
with the sound of my voice
tempered by the rhythm
of your breath

An Invitation to Father

for Robert Bly

I have dreamed all morning
watching the flowers bloom
will you come over and eat with me
the table is set
there is little else to do
except look at the garden and wait for you
the blossoms will not last long
please hurry
we must eat
wake up
and put the dishes away

Mortality

My song is thin
threadbare
as if I stepped through that memory
and sat with the odor of death
in the emptying room of my heart
it is early autumn
leaves fall slowly
one at a time
these words hardly pile up
before they blow away

Settling In

I have heard the dream
knocking
every night
every day
it is outside the window
behind the eyes
inside the house
trapped
in the heart
awake or asleep
knocking
it is not that I lack courage
I have just gotten used
to the rhythm
the slow steady beat
of keeping myself
at bay

The Carpenter

He works through the day
caressing the wood as so much familiar flesh
as if his hands carry him
he wonders what it is they want
perhaps he was once a tree
his feet so willing to plant roots
but his hands
nervous as small branches
dream only of flight

ABOUT THE AUTHOR

Kevin Patrick Sullivan was born in 1954 and raised in Dearborn Heights, Michigan, a west side suburb of Detroit. After graduating high school in 1972, he traveled the great American freeways and backroads between Michigan, Florida, and California. In 1975 he settled on the central coast of California in Shell Beach. For 18 years he lived in a small house with acreage adjacent to the Pacific Ocean, furthering his education.

In 1982 Kevin self-published his first book of poems and stepped out into the world of poetry. In 1984 he co-founded the annual San Luis Obispo Poetry Festival and Corners of the Mouth, a monthly reading series at Linnaea's Cafe in San Luis Obispo. In April 1992, he founded The Excellent Series, a monthly reading at the Excellent Center for Arts & Culture in Grover Beach. He is currently director of all three programs. Kevin lives in San Luis Obispo and works as a night custodian for the local school district.